COOKING
THE
THAI
WAY

This book is available in two editions:
Library binding by Lerner Publications Company,
    a division of Lerner Publishing Group
Soft cover by First Avenue Editions,
    an imprint of Lerner Publishing Group
241 First Avenue North
Minneapolis, MN 55401 U.S.A.

Website address: www.lernerbooks.com

Library of Congress Cataloging-in-Publication Data

Harrison, Supenn.
    Cooking the Thai way / by Supenn Harrison & Judy Monroe—Rev. & expanded.
        p.   cm. — (Easy menu ethnic cookbooks)
    Includes index.
    Summary: An introduction to the cooking of Thailand including such recipes as lemon chicken soup, satay, and Thai spring rolls. Also includes information on the history, geography, customs, and people of Thailand.
    ISBN: 0-8225-4124-6 (lib. bdg.: alk. paper)
    ISBN: 0-8225-0608-4 (pbk.: alk. paper)
    1. Cookery, Thai—Juvenile literature. 2. Thailand—Social life and customs—Juvenile literature. [1. Cookery, Thai. 2. Thailand—Social life and customs.] I. Judy Monroe. II. Title. III. Series.
TX724.5.T5 H37 2003   2001005485
641.59593—dc21

Manufactured in the United States of America
1 2 3 4 5 6 – AM – 08 07 06 05 04 03

COOKING

THE

revised and expanded

THAI

to include new low-fat

WAY

and vegetarian recipes

Supenn Harrison & Judy Monroe

Lerner Publications Company • Minneapolis

Contents

Introduction

Unique is the word for the cooking of Thailand. Thai food is wonderful to smell, exciting to see, and delicious to eat. The flavors of Thai cooking range from mild to almost searingly hot, with plenty of dishes falling somewhere in between. Many Thai consider food to be an art form. They have borrowed and adapted ideas from other countries to create their own distinctive cuisine.

Rice is grown in abundance in Thailand's fertile valleys. A big bowl of fluffy white rice is the center of most Thai meals. Spicy soups and curries in sauces are added to the rice to give it flavor. Main dishes of meat, vegetables, and herbs are put atop the rice to give it texture and nutrition.

Thai people are masters at mixing and matching food flavors and textures. They balance sweet flavors with sour, smooth foods with crunchy ones, and salty ingredients with hot ones.

As the Thai have traveled the world for study, business, or pleasure, they have introduced the flavors they adore to others. Cities around the world have Thai eating places, and the unique Thai flavors have become very popular.

Floating merchants sell their produce on a canal in Bangkok, the capital of Thailand.

The Land and Its People

Thailand is a nation, about the size of France, located in Southeast Asia. It is surrounded by land on all but its southern end, where it borders the Gulf of Thailand on the east and the Andaman Sea on the west. Myanmar (formerly Burma) lies to the north and west, while Laos and Cambodia (also called Kampuchea) share Thailand's eastern border. Thailand's neighbor to the south is Malaysia, which forms the tip of the Malay Peninsula.

Thailand is made up of four very different regions. The Northern Mountain region in the northwest is a rugged land of thick forests and steep mountains, crisscrossed by many rivers. The Central Plain, a flat, broad expanse dominated by the mighty Chao Phraya River, is the country's most heavily populated region. This fertile plain is nicknamed the Rice Bowl of Asia for its large exports of high-quality rice. East of the Central Plain is the Khorat Plateau, a large, dry region with sandy soil. The Southern Peninsula, which borders the western side of the Gulf of Thailand, is mostly tropical rain forest. The climate in Thailand is very hot and very humid. Daytime temperatures can reach 86°F.

The vast majority of the Thai people are farmers who live in rural areas. Thailand has few large cities. The capital city of Bangkok, located in the Central Plain on the Gulf of Thailand, is the country's largest and most modern city, with a population of over six million. Bangkok was once called the Venice of the East because of its canals, or *klongs*, but the city has grown so rapidly that many of the klongs have been filled in to make room for buildings and highways. Other large cities in Thailand are Hat Yai and Songkhla in the south and Nakhon Ratchasima in the northeast. Chiang Mai, the unofficial northern capital of Thailand, is internationally known for its exquisite handicrafts.

The Thai have never been ruled by a Western nation and are very proud of their independence. However, they are also open to ideas from other countries. They are masters at blending the old with the new to create something that is unmistakably Thai.

This talent for adaptation is most apparent in the arts, which have shown a great deal of Indian and, most recently, Western influence. The Thai are known the world over for their elaborate flower arrangements, fine handicrafts, and beautifully woven silks.

Most Thai are Buddhists. They follow the teachings of Siddhartha Gautama, or the Buddha. This Indian sage and philosopher lived more than two thousand years ago. Most Buddhist males become monks for a period of months sometime during their lives. As

A table is set with offerings to the gods at the Wat Po Temple in Bangkok.

monks, they shave their heads, wear traditional yellow robes, and live dependent on the charity of others. Buddhists who want to "make merit"—earn merit by doing good deeds—serve freshly cooked foods to monks who come to their doors in the morning. (Monks never eat anything after noon.) A Buddhist temple, with its elaborate roof and statue of the Buddha, is the center of most Thai villages. Informally, Thailand is called the Land of Smiles because the people tend to be happy and are often smiling.

History

The earliest Thai people migrated from the Chinese province of Yunnan in the A.D. 1200s. They had been called Ta'i, meaning "free," since the first century. By the mid-1300s, the Thai controlled most of what would become Thailand. This area had been called Sayam, so the people were called Siamese. They established a central government and made Ayutthaya the capital.

The Siamese fought border wars almost continuously from the 1300s to the 1600s. In 1767 Burma (later called Myanmar) captured and completely destroyed Ayutthaya, but the Siamese were not defeated. By 1777 the Burmese had been driven out and a new capital had been established at Thonburi. In 1782 General Chakri became King Rama I and moved the capital to Bangkok.

During the second half of the 1800s, the Siamese were ruled by two very popular and influential kings, Rama IV and Rama V. These men, who were father and son, are remembered for their social reforms. In 1932 a bloodless revolution ended the king's absolute power, and a constitutional monarchy was established with both a king and a prime minister. In 1939, just before World War II, the government decided to drop the name Siam and become Thailand. The country remained neutral during the war.

Thailand is located in a region undergoing economic recovery from the lengthy Vietnam War of the mid-1900s. However, Thailand is one of the most prosperous and stable countries in Southeast Asia. The Thai people are united in their love and respect for their king and are proud to be the "Free People."

The Food

Thai cooks insist on using only the freshest and best quality ingredients. Their food is spicy and rich with a characteristic blend of sweet, sour, and salty tastes, and it is usually beautifully arranged.

Over the years, Thai cuisine has been greatly influenced by other countries. But, whatever a recipe's origin, the Thai seem to be able to make it uniquely and deliciously their own. Chinese and Indian influences are especially strong in Thai cuisine. Stir-frying is a popular cooking technique that was adopted from China. Many Thai dishes have Chinese counterparts, which is not surprising because the original Thai came from southern China.

Indian influence on Thai cooking is most apparent in the curries, which are found in both cuisines. Although Thai curries are based on Indian curries, they are not the same because the Thai have substituted their own herbs and spices. Another similarity is the use of coconut milk with curries and with other dishes to mellow the flavors of the spices.

Thailand's terrain has isolated the four main regions of the country, to some degree, and the cuisine of each region has its own unique characteristics. Grilled foods with wonderful, rich sauces are very popular in northeastern Thailand. Like their Laotian neighbors, Thai from this region prefer short-grained sticky rice to the long-grained rice that is common throughout the rest of Thailand. The central Thai are famous for their spicy cuisine, while those from the north prefer milder dishes. Fresh fish and shellfish from the Gulf of Thailand are favorites of the southern Thai. The south also has a huge range of curries, and chilies (hot peppers) are eaten at every meal.

Herbs, spices, and sauces are the key ingredients in the cooking of every region in Thailand. The Thai flavor their food with black pepper, lemon juice, curry powder or curry paste, basil leaves, lemon grass, cilantro, ginger root, and garlic. (Lemon grass is often grown in pots on a family's kitchen windowsill, where it is handy for cooking.) Sauces include oyster sauce, soy sauce, and fish sauce.

The Thai use only a fork and a spoon for eating. Since they do not use knives at mealtime, meats and vegetables are always cut into bite-sized pieces before serving.

Due to the extreme heat in Thailand, cooling beverages are always at hand. For quick energy, fresh pineapple and sugarcane stalks are crushed for juice. Limeade, lemonade, and orangeade offer cooling refreshment, as do drinks based on coconut milk. Villagers also enjoy "tead" ice, which is made by freezing tea, then crushing the frozen tea and sipping it from a glass.

Holidays and Festivals

The Thai people love having fun. The Thai have a word for it: *sanuk*, the art of having fun. Making merry on holidays and festivals is an important part of life.

The King's Birthday is a national holiday, and on that day, each town is decorated with strings of colored lights. At night families walk around and try to find the most spectacular decorations. In celebration of the King's Birthday, the dinner table is filled with traditional dishes and family favorites. A typical meal might be steamed whole chicken with a hot pepper dipping sauce plus sliced roast pig's head, also served with dipping sauce. Another festive day, also celebrated with strings of lights and favorite foods, is the Queen's Birthday.

Some Thai celebrate the New Year not once but three times every year. They observe New Year's Day on the first of January. Thai who have Chinese ancestors enjoy the Chinese New Year, which comes on the first day of the first Chinese lunar month (usually in February). This is a three-day holiday when businesses close and extended families get together. Many Thai also celebrate the old Thai New Year, called Songkran, in April.

In Thailand the New Year's table is decorated with exquisite arrangements of many kinds of tropical fruit, including bananas, coconuts, pineapples, and papayas. New Year's is also the time to eat delicious Thai spring rolls with *nam pla prig*, a flavorful sauce. Serving brown eggs at New Year's is a unique tradition in some Thai families. The hard-boiled eggs are cooked in soy sauce, sugar, fish sauce, and five spices. The eggs symbolize a good life in the coming year.

Songkran is a three-day water festival marking the old Thai New

Year in mid-April. Since April is the hottest month in Thailand, celebrating this holiday is very refreshing and lots of fun. People douse each other with water and wash everything thoroughly to symbolize washing away any sins or bad luck of the past year. Pouring on water is also a way of giving thanks for the rains and asking for good luck in the coming year. Everyone wears light, easy-to-dry clothing, knowing that water may be thrown at them many times during the day. When older people come along, water is poured only over their hands, not their heads, as a sign of respect.

During Songkran, families and friends gather for a huge feast. The meal always includes curries—usually yellow, the holiday color in Thailand. Long noodles that symbolize long life are also served. *Pad thai* is a popular dish made by frying the long rice noodles with meats and vegetables. A finger food often made during Songkran is *ma hore*, which means "galloping horses."

Another favorite holiday in Thailand is Loy Krathong, which is celebrated in November. Each year children and adults alike make small bamboo boats and put lighted candles inside them. Then they set the little boats afloat down a river. The Thai believe that the little boats carry away bad deeds. After the boats have been launched, a large meal is served. It includes grilled chicken, fish, coconut, and egg yolks (another yellow holiday food).

While holidays such as the King's Birthday and Songkran are celebrated all over Thailand, other festivals and fairs are local or regional. Many town celebrations are organized around religious and agricultural festivals. The Rambutan Fair in August in Surat Thani, not far from Thailand's border with Malaysia, is typical of these local fairs. The rambutan is a tropical fruit with a spiky bright red outside and juicy white fruit inside. The first trees were planted in Surat Thani in 1926 and grow all over the area. As part of the fair, floats are trimmed with rambutan and other fruits, and trained monkeys demonstrate how they can climb up and harvest the coconuts from coconut palms. A rambutan dessert is served that day.

Another colorful local fair is the Food and Fruits Fair in

September in Nakhon Pathom in southwestern Thailand near Bangkok. Fairgoers can learn new food combinations by watching expert cooks preparing Thai and Chinese foods. Many kinds of fruits are on display, including some of the nearly two dozen types of bananas that grow in Thailand.

Residents of Phuket, deep in southern Thailand, who have Chinese ancestors, eat no meat during their annual Phuket Vegetarian Festival. For ten days in the fall, Chinese Thai live on fruits, vegetables, greens, and grains. They use tofu and wild mushrooms in place of meat. Parades and religious ceremonies honor Chinese immigrants who came to the area in the 1800s.

Thailand's popular king and queen oversee the Royal Ploughing Ceremony in Bangkok during May. The ceremony celebrates the start of the rice planting season. In a way, the Thai celebrate rice every day of their lives, eating it at nearly every meal. Whatever the special occasion, the Thai celebrate with family and good food!

Dancers launch small, lit boats at a Loy Krathong festival at the Rose Garden in Nakhon Pathom.

Before You Begin

Cooking any dish, plain or fancy, is easier and more fun if you are familiar with its ingredients. Thai cooking calls for some ingredients that you may not know. Sometimes special cookware is also used, although the recipes in this book can easily be prepared with ordinary utensils and pans.

The most important thing you need to know before you start is how to be a careful cook. On the following page, you'll find a few rules that will make your cooking experience safe, fun, and easy. Next, take a look at the "dictionary" of utensils, terms, and special ingredients. You may also want to read the section on preparing healthy, low-fat meals for yourself, your family, and your friends.

Once you've picked out a recipe to try, read through it from beginning to end. Then you are ready to shop for ingredients and to organize the cookware you need. When you have assembled everything, you're ready to begin cooking.

Galloping horses (bottom) and tropical fruit dessert (top) are delicious foods to be eaten at holiday time or anytime. (Recipes on pages 66 and 67.)

The Careful Cook

Whenever you cook, there are certain safety rules you must always keep in mind. Even experienced cooks follow these rules when they are in the kitchen.

- Always wash your hands before handling food. Thoroughly wash all raw vegetables and fruits to remove dirt, chemicals, and insecticides. Wash uncooked poultry, fish, and meat under cold water.
- Use a cutting board when cutting up vegetables and fruits. Don't cut them up in your hand! And be sure to cut in a direction *away* from you and your fingers.
- Long hair or loose clothing can easily catch fire if brought near the burners of a stove. If you have long hair, tie it back before you start cooking.
- Turn all pot handles toward the back of the stove so that you will not catch your sleeves or jewelry on them. This is especially important when younger brothers and sisters are around. They could easily knock off a pot and get burned.
- Always use a pot holder to steady hot pots or to take pans out of the oven. Don't use a wet cloth on a hot pan because the steam it produces could burn you.
- Lift the lid of a steaming pot with the opening away from you so that you will not get burned.
- If you get burned, hold the burn under cold running water. Do not put grease or butter on it. Cold water helps to take the heat out, but grease or butter will only keep it in.
- If grease or cooking oil catches fire, throw baking soda or salt at the bottom of the flame to put it out. (Water will *not* put out a grease fire.) Call for help, and try to turn all the stove burners to "off."

- Chilies, such as the jalapeño peppers used in Asian cooking, must be handled with care. They contain oils that can burn your eyes and mouth. To be extra cautious, wear rubber gloves while fixing chilies. The way you cut the fresh chili peppers affects their "hotness." If you take out the seeds, the flavor will be sharp but not fiery. If you leave the seeds in, beware! After working with chilies, be sure not to touch your face until you have washed your hands thoroughly with soap and water.

Cooking Utensils

pastry brush—A small brush used for coating food with liquids

skewer—A thin wood or bamboo stick used to hold small pieces of meat or vegetables for broiling or grilling

wok—A pot with a rounded bottom and sloping sides, ideally suited for stir-frying dishes. A large skillet is a fine substitute.

Cooking Terms

boil—To heat a liquid over high heat until bubbles form and rise rapidly to the surface

broil—To cook directly under a heat source so that the side of the food facing the heat cooks rapidly

fillet—A boneless piece of fish or meat

grill—To cook over hot charcoal

simmer—To cook over low heat in liquid kept just below its boiling point

stir-fry—To cook bite-sized pieces of food in a small amount of oil over high heat, stirring and frying quickly

Special Ingredients

basil—A rich and fragrant herb whose leaves are used in cooking. The many varieties include Thai or holy basil, which has purplish stems.

bean sprouts—Sprouts from the mung bean. For best flavor and texture, use fresh sprouts.

black mushrooms—Dried, fragrant mushrooms available at Asian groceries. Black mushrooms are sometimes labeled black fungi.

cayenne pepper—A hot, pungent powder made from dried tropical chili peppers. Cayenne pepper may also be labeled red pepper.

cellophane noodles—Fine, clear, thin noodles made from mung beans. They are also called mung bean threads or transparent noodles and are sold in bundles.

chilies—Small red or green hot peppers used for seasoning. The smaller the chili pepper, the hotter the taste.

cilantro—Another name for fresh coriander (see definition below)

coconut milk—The white, milky liquid extracted from coconut meat, used to give a coconut flavor to foods. Regular and lite (reduced-fat) coconut milk are available canned in large supermarkets.

collard greens—A dark green, leafy plant that gives crunchy texture and valuable vitamins to main dishes, vegetable combinations, and salads

coriander—A leafy herb, also known as cilantro or Chinese parsley. The leaves have a strong flavor and a distinctive aroma. Ground coriander, made from dried seeds, adds spice to curries.

curry powder—A mixture of up to twenty herbs, seeds, and spices. It is usually yellow due to the turmeric that is added to the chilies, garlic, pepper, fennel, and other herbs.

extra-long-grain rice—A type of rice with large grains. It is dry and fluffy when cooked.

fish sauce—A fragrant bottled sauce made of processed fish, water, and salt. It adds a sweet-salty flavor to many Thai dishes and is available at Asian groceries and many supermarkets.

ginger root—A knobby, light brown root, which is grated or sliced to add a peppery, slightly sweet flavor to foods. To prepare fresh ginger root, use the side of a spoon to peel skin off a section and use a grater to grate the amount called for. Freeze the rest of the root for future use. Do not substitute dried ground ginger in a recipe calling for fresh ginger, as the taste is very different.

jalapeño pepper—A two-inch-long dark green chili pepper that makes food hot to very hot. It is available fresh and canned.

lemon grass—A tropical grass that grows in a long, slim bunch. The lower, white part of each stalk is chopped to add a strong lemon flavor to foods. Since lemon grass is very fibrous, it is best to remove chunks of it from food after cooking and before serving. If fresh lemon grass is not available, use chopped or grated lemon peel for desired lemon flavor. Though dried lemon grass is available, its use is not satisfactory.

lychee (or litchi)—A popular fruit with a spiky red shell and sweet, juicy, creamy-white flesh. The fruit is sold canned and fresh.

mango—A tropical fruit shaped like a kidney with orange gold tart-sweet flesh and yellow skin streaked with red

mint—The leaves of various mint plants are used in cooking and for a garnish. Due to its bright color and distinctive flavor, fresh mint is much preferred to dried.

papaya—A pear-shaped tropical fruit with yellow skin and sweet, juicy, yellow orange flesh

rambutan—A sweet, white tropical fruit much like the lychee. It is available canned in Asian markets and large supermarkets.

rice noodles—Very thin noodles made from rice. The packages may be labeled rice sticks or Oriental noodles and are available at Asian markets and some supermarkets.

tofu—A processed curd made from soybeans, which are an important protein source in Asia. Sold in blocks labeled soft, silken, or firm, tofu may be labeled soybean curd or bean curd.

Healthy and Low-Fat Cooking Tips

Many modern cooks are concerned about preparing healthy, low-fat meals. Fortunately, Thai cooking is healthy to start with since it calls for lots of fresh vegetables and fruits and smaller amounts of meat and oil.

When adapting recipes, it's best to make a recipe just the way it's printed the first time in order to get the flavor and texture right. Then, the next time you make the recipe, try substituting. Throughout the book, you'll also find specific suggestions for individual recipes—and don't worry, they'll still taste delicious!

Coconut milk is quite high in saturated fat. But it is frequently used in Thai cooking to cool the heat of spices and chilies. Try using a mixture of 1 cup whole milk or fat-free half-and-half plus ½ teaspoon imitation coconut extract in place of 1 cup of coconut milk.

For recipes calling for beef, chicken, or pork, use a sharp knife to cut off excess fat. Some cooks like to replace ground beef with ground turkey to lower fat. However, since this does change the flavor, you may need to experiment a little bit to decide if you like this substitution. Buying extra lean ground beef is also an easy way to reduce fat. And when directions say that the wok or skillet should be heated and coated with oil before stir-frying, use a low-fat vegetable oil spray to coat the pan.

Thai cooking often calls for soy sauce, a seasoning that, like salt, adds a great deal of flavor but is high in sodium. To lower the sodium content in a recipe, try reducing the amount of soy sauce. You can also substitute lite (low-sodium) soy sauce. Be aware that soy sauce labeled "light" is usually only lighter in color than regular soy sauce, not lower in sodium nor as thick or intense in flavor.

There are many ways to prepare meals that are good for you and still taste great. As you become a more experienced cook, try experimenting with recipes and substitutions to find the methods that work for you.

METRIC CONVERSIONS

Cooks in the United States measure both liquid and solid ingredients using standard containers based on the 8-ounce cup and the tablespoon. These measurements are based on volume, while the metric system of measurement is based on both weight (for solids) and volume (for liquids). To convert from U.S. fluid tablespoons, ounces, quarts, and so forth to metric liters is a straightforward conversion, using the chart below. However, since solids have different weights—one cup of rice does not weigh the same as one cup of grated cheese, for example—many cooks who use the metric system have kitchen scales to weigh different ingredients. The chart below will give you a good starting point for basic conversions to the metric system.

MASS (weight)

1 ounce (oz.)	=	28.0 grams (g)
8 ounces	=	227.0 grams
1 pound (lb.) or 16 ounces	=	0.45 kilograms (kg)
2.2 pounds	=	1.0 kilogram

LIQUID VOLUME

1 teaspoon (tsp.)	=	5.0 milliliters (ml)
1 tablespoon (tbsp.)	=	15.0 milliliters
1 fluid ounce (oz.)	=	30.0 milliliters
1 cup (c.)	=	240 milliliters
1 pint (pt.)	=	480 milliliters
1 quart (qt.)	=	0.95 liters (l)
1 gallon (gal.)	=	3.80 liters

LENGTH

¼ inch (in.)	=	0.6 centimeters (cm)
½ inch	=	1.25 centimeters
1 inch	=	2.5 centimeters

TEMPERATURE

212°F	=	100°C (boiling point of water)
225°F	=	110°C
250°F	=	120°C
275°F	=	135°C
300°F	=	150°C
325°F	=	160°C
350°F	=	180°C
375°F	=	190°C
400°F	=	200°C

(To convert temperature in Fahrenheit to Celsius, subtract 32 and multiply by .56)

PAN SIZES

8-inch cake pan	= 20 x 4-centimeter cake pan
9-inch cake pan	= 23 x 3.5-centimeter cake pan
11 x 7-inch baking pan	= 28 x 18-centimeter baking pan
13 x 9-inch baking pan	= 32.5 x 23-centimeter baking pan
9 x 5-inch loaf pan	= 23 x 13-centimeter loaf pan
2-quart casserole	= 2-liter casserole

A Thai Table

Just as the Thai wear Western-style clothing rather than traditional costume, so the Thai are steadily moving toward the Western way of serving meals: at a table. The traditional Thai meal is served on the floor. In ordinary homes, members of the family and guests kneel in a circle on mats. Well-to-do hosts arrange pillows for family and friends to kneel on while eating.

Whether the meal is served on the floor or at a table, Thai cooks plan one main dish per person, plus rice. For example, if there were four in the family and one child invited a school friend, there would be five dishes, plus rice. One of the dishes would always be a soup or a curry to moisten the rice. All main dishes are served at once.

Since the Thai love brilliant color, the table or the room around it might be decorated with the many tropical flowers—even orchids—that grow everywhere in this hot country. A basket of fruits could also be part of the food offering. Each dish, no matter how simple, is always carefully cooked and arranged so it is as attractive as it is delicious.

In Thailand some families eat their meals on the floor.

A Thai Menu

The Thai eat three meals a day—breakfast, lunch, and dinner—plus snacks of fruits, soups, noodle dishes, and sweets. The focal point of each meal is plenty of hot, fragrant rice. Breakfast often includes boiled eggs, fried rice, and leftovers from the previous day's dinner. A noodle dish served with stir-fried vegetables is a typical lunch. Dinner usually consists of fresh salads, a dip or sauce, soup or curry, and side dishes of steamed, fried, or stir-fried vegetables with meat, fish, chicken, or seafood.

When planning a Thai meal, try to balance hot, mild, salty, sweet, and sour flavors. Remember that rice will cool the stinging bite of chilies.

Below are menu plans and shopping lists for a lunch and a dinner. All the recipes are found in this book.

LUNCH

Thai fried rice

Cucumber salad

Fresh fruit

SHOPPING LIST:

Produce

1 onion
1 head garlic
1 tomato
1 bunch green onions
6 cherry tomatoes or 2 Roma
  tomatoes
2 cucumbers
1 lime or lemon
1 bunch fresh cilantro
Bananas
Mangoes
Papaya

Dairy/Egg/Meat

2 eggs
1 lb. pork loin

Canned/Bottled/Boxed

extra-long-grain rice
fish sauce
vegetable oil

Miscellaneous

black pepper
red (cayenne) pepper flakes
granulated white sugar

DINNER

Rice

Lemon chicken soup

Stir-fried meat with basil

Stir-fried vegetables

Thai coconut custard

SHOPPING LIST:

Produce

1 bulb lemon grass or 1 lemon
1 c. fresh cauliflower
1 tomato
1 lb. fresh mushrooms
1 head garlic
1 onion
1 bunch fresh basil
1 small winter squash (such as acorn squash)
2 jalapeño peppers
2 c. assorted vegetables for stir-frying: 1 green, such as broccoli or snow peas; 1 white, such as cabbage or bean sprouts; and 1 yellow orange, such as carrots or winter squash

Dairy/Egg/Meat

4 eggs
10 oz. skinless, boneless chicken breast halves
1 lb. beef sirloin tip

Canned/Bottled/Boxed

extra-long-grain rice
2 10¾-oz. cans chicken broth
1 14-oz. can coconut milk, or 1 c. unsweetened shredded coconut
fish sauce
lemon juice
vegetable oil

Miscellaneous

granulated white sugar
brown sugar
pepper

Rice and More

Many varieties of rice are grown in Thailand. In fact, the Thai saying for a stroke of good luck is to have "fallen into the rice bowl." Short-grained sticky rice is often eaten by the central and northeastern Thai. Another especially delicious variety is jasmine, or fragrant, rice. A big serving dish of hot, fluffy white rice is always in the center of the other foods on the table, whether for breakfast, lunch, or dinner. In fact, all the dishes on the table, soups or curries, stir-fries or salads, are called *gap kao*, meaning "with rice."

Chicken soup and beef curry are typical of the saucy main dishes that add flavor and liquid to plain rice. Diners usually add a little of each of the foods offered to their rice for the first plate, then go back for a second portion of their favorites.

Soups can be sour or "mixed." Sour soups include lemon grass and lemon juice and sometimes lemon leaves. Mixed soups often have more ingredients than sour soups and include meat, poultry, or seafood, and vegetables. Thrifty cooks make delicious soups from inexpensive vegetables, such as cabbage and onions, and from cheap meats, such as fish heads.

Curries are the specialty of southern Thailand, where chilies are included in every meal. Curries often include coconut milk for a sweeter and milder taste.

Lemon chicken soup (bottom) makes a tasty sauce for rice (top). (Recipes on pages 30 and 31.)

Rice / Kow

The backbone of every Thai meal is extra-long-grain rice. The directions below will produce rice that is fluffy but rather dry, ready to soak up lots of soup or curry during the meal.

2 c. extra-long-grain rice

2 ½ c. water

1. In a deep saucepan, bring rice and water to a boil over high heat. Boil, uncovered, for 2 to 3 minutes.

2. Cover pan and reduce heat to low. Simmer rice 20 to 25 minutes, or until all water is absorbed.

3. Remove pan from heat. Keep covered and let rice steam for 10 minutes.

4. Fluff rice with a fork and serve hot.*

Preparation time: 5 minutes
Cooking time: 33 to 38 minutes
Makes 6 cups

* Leftover rice freezes well. Package it in 1- or 2-cup amounts in freezer-ready, zipper-style plastic bags.

Lemon Chicken Soup / Tom Chude Gai Ma Noun

The Thai love sharp flavors, and this popular soup, served throughout the country, satisfies with its delicious lemony tang. Shrimp, fish, or crab can be substituted for the chicken.

2 10 ¾-oz. cans (about 3 c.) chicken broth

1 stalk lemon grass, bottom one-third cut into 1-inch pieces, or 1 tbsp. grated lemon peel

10 oz. boneless, skinless chicken breast halves, cut into ¾-inch pieces

1 c. bite-sized pieces fresh cauliflower, or 1 c. frozen chopped cauliflower, thawed

1 tomato, cut into 8 wedges

½ c. sliced fresh mushrooms, or 1 3-oz. can sliced mushrooms, drained*

1 tsp. sugar

2 tbsp. fish sauce

1½ tbsp. lemon juice

1. In a large saucepan, bring broth to a boil over high heat. Add lemon grass and reduce heat to medium. Cook, uncovered, for 5 minutes, or until broth has a lemon taste.

2. Add chicken, cauliflower, tomato, and mushrooms. Cook uncovered for 3 or 4 minutes, or until chicken and cauliflower are tender.

3. Add sugar, fish sauce, and lemon juice. Stir well.

4. Serve hot over rice, or in individual soup bowls with rice on the side.

Preparation time: 15 to 20 minutes
Cooking time: 10 to 12 minutes
Serves 4

* If you wish, a 4-oz. can of mushroom stems and pieces, drained, can be used in place of the 3-oz. can of sliced mushrooms.

Panaeng Beef Curry / Panaeng Nua

Panaeng, a thick curry that does not include vegetables, originated in Malaysia. It can be made with either chicken or beef.

2 c. coconut milk (see recipe page 36)

1 lb. stewing beef, cut into bite-sized pieces

1 clove garlic, finely chopped

¼ tsp. ground coriander

⅛ tsp. pepper

¼ tsp. salt

1 stalk lemon grass, bottom one-third finely chopped

3 tbsp. fish sauce

½ tsp. lemon rind, finely chopped

2 tbsp. chunky peanut butter

1 tbsp. sugar

½ tbsp. crushed red pepper flakes

1 green onion, minced

basil leaves or sliced red chilies for garnish

1. In a large saucepan, bring coconut milk to a boil over high heat, stirring occasionally. Reduce heat to low and simmer, uncovered, for 15 minutes, stirring occasionally.

2. Add remaining ingredients and stir. Cover and simmer over medium heat, stirring occasionally, for 1½ to 2 hours, or until beef is tender.

3. Serve hot over rice. Garnish with basil or sliced red chilies.

Preparation time: 15 to 20 minutes
Cooking time: 2 to 2½ hours
Serves 4

Noodle Dishes

In Thailand noodles are usually served at lunch. Busy vendors sell delicious noodle dishes on the streets all over Thailand. The noodles are not cut because long noodles are a sign of good luck.

Noodles made of rice are popular in Thailand and can be added to soups or to stir-fried, steamed, or simmered dishes, including curries. Very thin egg noodles are also eaten, as are cellophane noodles, which are made from mung beans. Noodles provide the something soft and something bland that balance the crunchy and/or spicy foods in the Thai kitchen. Noodles work well in many foods, such as Thai spring rolls (recipe on pages 58–59).

Pineapple-fish noodles (recipe on page 37) are made of two of Thailand's most popular foods: pineapples and fish. Many different types of fish may be used in this dish to add variety.

Rice Noodles/ *Guay Teow*

3 c. water

½ package (14 oz. or 16 oz.) rice
   noodles

1. In a large saucepan, bring water to a boil over high heat. Add rice noodles and return water to a boil.

2. Reduce heat to medium-high and cook noodles, uncovered, for 4 to 5 minutes, or until soft.

3. Drain noodles and rinse in cold water. Serve immediately.

Preparation time: 5 minutes
Cooking time: 5 minutes
Serves 4

Coconut Milk

Coconut milk is a must for curries, sauces, and desserts. Unsweetened coconut is sold at health food stores, food co-ops, and some large supermarkets. If you don't have time to make your own coconut milk, use canned coconut milk instead.

2 c. unsweetened dried coconut

3 c. boiling water

1. Put coconut into electric blender. Pour boiling water over coconut. Cover blender. Blend at medium speed for 30 seconds.

2. Place a fine sieve over a medium bowl. Pour coconut mixture into sieve. Press coconut with a large spoon to squeeze out all milk.

3. Chill any leftover coconut milk and use it within three days.

Preparation time: 15 minutes
Makes 2 cups

Pineapple-Fish Noodles / Ka Nom Jeen Sour Nam

Pineapple has been popular in Thailand for hundreds of years. The Thai love its sweet-sour taste and often use it in cooked dishes.

3 tbsp. vegetable oil

2 lb. fish fillets, cut into bite-sized pieces*

1 clove garlic, finely chopped**

1 tsp. grated fresh ginger

1 20-oz. can crushed pineapple, drained thoroughly

1 c. coconut milk (recipe on page 36)

2 tsp. fish sauce

1/8 tsp. pepper

1 tsp. sugar

1/8 tsp. cayenne pepper

hot rice noodles (recipe on page 36)

fresh mint and cilantro for garnish (optional)

1. In a large skillet or wok, heat oil over high heat for 1 minute.

2. Add fish, garlic, and ginger. Cook, stirring constantly, for 3 minutes, or until fish becomes white.

3. Add pineapple, coconut milk, fish sauce, pepper, sugar, and cayenne pepper and stir well. Cook, stirring constantly, for 2 minutes, or until fish flakes easily.

4. Serve over hot rice noodles. Garnish with fresh mint and cilantro.

Preparation time: 30 minutes
Cooking time: 10 minutes
Serves 6 to 8

* For this recipe, orange roughy, whitefish, trout, red snapper, sole, cod, haddock, or any other mild flaky-textured fish can be used.

** When you chop garlic, add a little salt. That way, the garlic doesn't stick to the knife as much. Since the salt absorbs the garlic juice, no flavor is lost.

Beef Noodles / Guay Teow Nua

3 dried black mushrooms

1½ tsp. cornstarch

¼ c. chicken broth or water

3 tbsp. vegetable oil

1 lb. beef sirloin tip, thinly sliced

½ medium onion, peeled and thinly sliced

1 clove garlic, finely chopped

2 c. fresh broccoli, chopped, or 2 c. frozen chopped broccoli, thawed

1 tsp. soy sauce

1 tsp. fish sauce

⅛ tsp. pepper

hot rice noodles (recipe on page 36), or egg noodles to serve 4

1. In a small bowl, soak black mushrooms in hot water for 15 minutes. Drain well in a colander and shred, discarding the stems.

2. In another small bowl, stir together cornstarch and broth. Set aside.

3. In a large skillet or wok, heat 2 tbsp. oil over high heat for 1 minute. Add meat and cook, stirring constantly, for 2 to 3 minutes, or until beef is tender and nearly all brown. Place meat in a bowl and set aside.

4. Wash skillet or wok and dry thoroughly. Heat 1 tbsp. oil in wok over high heat for 1 minute. Add onion and garlic and cook, stirring constantly, for 2 minutes until nearly tender.

5. Add broccoli and stir well. Stir cornstarch-broth mixture and add to vegetables. Cover, reduce heat to low, and simmer for 2 to 3 minutes, or until broccoli is crisp-tender.

6. Add mushrooms, soy sauce, fish sauce, pepper, and meat. Cook, stirring frequently, for 1 to 2 minutes, or until heated through.

7. Serve hot with noodles.

Preparation time: 15 to 20 minutes
Cooking time: 15 minutes
Serves 4

Easy Main Dishes

Thai food is healthy and delicious, yet quick and easy to prepare. Meats, vegetables, and fruits are cut up before cooking so that they cook quickly. This saves time and fuel and makes the foods easy to eat with just a fork and spoon as the Thai like to do.

Many favorite Thai foods are stir-fried. Stir-frying probably originated in China and was then borrowed by the Thai. You can use either a wide skillet or a Chinese wok for this very quick cooking method. Have your ingredients chopped, measured, and ready near the pan before you start to stir-fry.

Thai cooks also like to cook on a grill. Grilling is a cooking technique that the Thai may have learned from the people of Java (an island in Indonesia). If you do not have a charcoal grill, use your oven to broil or bake these foods.

Stir-fried meat with basil (bottom) and Thai fried rice (top) are delicious dishes made using the stir-fry technique. (Recipes on pages 42 and 43.)

Stir-Fried Meat with Basil/ Nua Bye Ga Pon

Thai cooks usually use holy basil in this quick and easy dish, which originated hundreds of years ago. Sweet basil is easier to find in the United States and is a good substitute. Chicken or shrimp can be used instead of beef. This salad is spicy, with tender meat and crunchy vegetables.

3 tbsp. vegetable oil

I lb. beef sirloin tip, thinly sliced

I clove garlic, finely chopped

½ medium onion, peeled and sliced

½ c. sliced fresh mushrooms, or
   I 3-oz. can sliced mushrooms,
   drained

2 jalapeño peppers, seeded and cut
   into quarters

I tbsp. fish sauce

I tsp. sugar

½ to I cup coarsely chopped fresh
   basil leaves*

* If fresh basil is not available, use 1
tbsp. dried basil leaves plus ½ c.
chopped fresh parsley.

1. In a large skillet or wok, heat 2 tbsp. oil over high heat for 1 minute. Add meat and cook over high heat, stirring constantly, until beef begins to turn brown. Place meat in a bowl and set aside.

2. Wash skillet or wok and dry thoroughly.

3. Heat remaining oil in skillet or wok over high heat for 1 minute. Add garlic, onion, mushrooms, and peppers and stir well. Cook, stirring frequently, for 1 minute, or until mushrooms and peppers are soft.

4. Add meat, fish sauce, and sugar and stir well. Cook, stirring constantly, over medium heat for 2 minutes, or until heated through.

5. Add basil, stir-fry just until leaves wilt (about 10 seconds).

6. Serve hot over rice.

Preparation time: 15 minutes
Cooking time: 10 minutes
Serves 4

Thai Fried Rice/Kow Pad Thai

The original Thai brought this dish from China, and it quickly became a favorite family dish—with Thai touches, of course. It is good for using up leftovers because a variety of vegetables and meats or shrimp can be substituted. Although fried rice is often served as a breakfast or lunch dish, it can become a party dish by adding 2 tbsp. of curry powder. The curry mixture includes turmeric, which colors food yellow. The Thai consider yellow to be a party or celebration color.

2 eggs

4 tbsp. vegetable oil

½ medium onion, peeled and chopped

1 lb. pork loin, thinly sliced*

1 clove garlic, finely chopped

1 tomato, sliced into 8 wedges

2 green onions, thinly sliced

1 tbsp. fish sauce (or soy sauce)

1 tsp. sugar

½ tsp. pepper

½ tsp. cayenne pepper (optional)

4 c. cold cooked rice

* To turn this recipe into a quick meatless meal, substitute 1 package firm tofu for pork. Cut tofu into ½ × 1-inch sticks and fry in the hot oil before scrambling the eggs in Step 2. Substitute soy sauce for the fish sauce.

1. In a small bowl, beat eggs well.

2. In a large skillet or wok, heat 1 tbsp. oil over medium heat for 1 minute. Add beaten eggs and scramble them. Place eggs on a plate and set aside.

3. Clean skillet or wok. Heat 3 tbsp. oil over medium heat for 1 minute. Add onions, pork, and garlic and stir well. Cook, uncovered, for 2 minutes, stirring occasionally.

4. Add tomato and green onions and cook, stirring occasionally, for 2 minutes, or until tomatoes soften.

5. Add fish sauce, sugar, pepper, and cayenne pepper and stir well.

6. Add rice, breaking apart any clumps. Mix well and cook, uncovered, for 6 to 8 minutes, or until heated through.

7. Add scrambled eggs and mix well.

Preparation time: 15 minutes
Cooking time: 15 minutes
Serves 4

Satay

This party dish is originally from Malaysia. The southern Thai add more curry, making the satay spicier. In northern Thailand, it is served with sticky rice and stir-fried vegetables.

2 tsp. sugar

1 tbsp. fish sauce

1½ tsp. curry powder

¼ tsp. pepper

1½ lb. pork loin, thinly sliced and cut into ½ x 2-inch strips

1½ c. coconut milk (recipe on page 36)

4 tbsp. chunky peanut butter

2 tsp. fish sauce

* Satay is delicious served with a cucumber salad (recipe on page 50) or with cucumber sauce (recipe on page 55).

1. In a large mixing bowl, combine the first 4 ingredients and mix well. Cover pork with fish sauce marinade and refrigerate for 4 hours or overnight.

2. In a deep saucepan, mix remaining ingredients. Bring to a boil over high heat, stirring constantly until well mixed. Place this coconut-peanut butter sauce in a bowl, cover, and refrigerate.

3. Soak 8- or 10-inch bamboo skewers in water for half an hour so they won't catch fire in the broiler.

4. Preheat oven to broil.

5. Thread pork onto skewers accordion style. When oven is preheated, broil pork for 8 to 10 minutes, or until done, turning often so all sides are cooked evenly.

6. Serve hot with bowls of the coconut-peanut butter sauce for dipping.

Preparation time: 20 to 30 minutes
(plus 4 hours for marinating)
Cooking time: 10 to 15 minutes
Serves 6

Satay (bottom), cucumber salad (top left), and rice (top right) make a tasty meal.

Grilled Marinated Chicken / Gai Yaang

In Thailand, pieces of meat, poultry, fish, and seafood are often grilled or broiled and served with a spicy dipping sauce.

3 tsp. sugar

2 tbsp. soy sauce

2 tbsp. fish sauce

I tsp. pepper

I clove garlic, finely chopped

I 2½- to 3-lb.chicken, cut into quarters

*When checking chicken for doneness, it's a good idea to cut it open gently to make sure the meat is white (not pink) all the way through.

1. Mix first 5 ingredients. Pour mixture over chicken in a large bowl. Cover and refrigerate for 4 hours or overnight.

2. With the help of an adult, place chicken on grill over hot coals with skin side up. Cook 10 minutes. Turn every 10 minutes until done, about 40 minutes in all. Chicken is done when juices run clear after flesh is pierced with a fork. If you prefer, broil chicken in preheated broiler 40 to 45 minutes, turning often so that all sides are cooked evenly. To bake chicken, place chicken in a baking dish in a 400°F oven. Bake 30 to 45 minutes.

3. Serve chicken with nam pla prig (recipe on page 54) or with sweet and sour sauce (recipe on page 55).

Preparation time: 10 minutes (plus 4 hours for marinating)
Cooking time: 40 to 45 minutes
Serves 4

Accompaniments

Thai cuisine is known for its combinations of sweet, sour, and salty flavors, which are created by adding herbs and seasonings to meats, fish, and tofu and vegetables. Popular herbs include basil, coriander, galangal (a milder tasting cousin of ginger), garlic, ginger, lemon grass, and lime leaves. Dips and sauces are planned to contrast with these key flavors. For example, a sweet and sour sauce of cooling cucumbers is the perfect accompaniment for pork satay. The cucumber sauce contrasts with the salty fish sauce and spicy curry flavors of the satay.

This chapter includes recipes for a variety of Thai dips and sauces that can be served as accompaniments for many dishes. The chapter also includes recipes for salads and for a stir-fry, all of which may be served as side dishes or as an accompaniment to rice, which the Thai consider to be the main food at any meal.

For a light meal or snack, try cucumber salad (top) or spinach salad with chicken (bottom). (Recipes on pages 50 and 51.)

Cucumber Salad / Sa-lat Tang Gua

This refreshing cucumber salad can be served with a meal or as a snack. It is a popular side dish with Thai spring rolls.

6 cherry tomatoes, halved, or 2 Roma tomatoes, diced

2 cucumbers, peeled, seeded, and coarsely shredded

2 green onions, finely chopped

2 tbsp. fish sauce

¼ tsp. crushed red pepper flakes*

2 tbsp. lime or lemon juice

2 tbsp. sugar

fresh cilantro for garnish (optional)

1. Combine all ingredients except cilantro in a large bowl. Lightly crush tomatoes and green onions with a large spoon and mix well.

2. Garnish salad with fresh cilantro. Serve cold or at room temperature. Drain off any excess liquid just before serving.

Preparation time: 15 minutes
Serves 4 to 6

*When cooking with red pepper flakes or ground red pepper, a little goes a long way. It is easy to add a little more red pepper when you want to and impossible to take it out when there's too much. Try adding 1/8 teaspoon of pepper flakes at a time, then tasting.

Spinach Salad with Chicken/ Sa-lat Pak Sa-pin-ach

Collard greens are a common ingredient in Thai cooking and are usually used in this salad. In the United States, spinach is often easier to find and will make a fine substitute. This party dish originated in the northeastern region of Thailand and is usually very spicy.

1 whole skinless chicken breast
  (about 10 oz.)

1½ tbsp. fish sauce

3 tbsp. sugar

3 tbsp. lime or lemon juice

⅛ tsp. cayenne pepper

3 c. chopped fresh spinach

½ c. chopped roasted peanuts

½ c. peeled and shredded carrots

1. Rinse chicken breast under cool running water. Place in a large saucepan with enough water to cover, and bring to a boil. Cover, reduce heat to low, and simmer for 30 minutes, or until tender.

2. Remove chicken from pan with tongs. Place on a plate and cool for 15 minutes. When chicken is cool, remove meat from bones and shred into small pieces. Place shredded chicken in a large bowl.

3. In a small bowl, mix fish sauce, sugar, lime juice, and cayenne. Mix until sugar dissolves.

4. Pour juice mixture over chicken and mix well.

5. Place spinach on a serving plate. Spoon chicken over spinach and top with peanuts and carrots. Serve at room temperature.

Preparation time: 15 minutes
Cooking time: 30 minutes (plus 15 minutes cooling time)
Serves 4

Stir-Fried Vegetables / Pad Pak

The Thai adopted the Chinese technique of stir-frying to preserve the color, fresh flavor, and texture of each vegetable. Only the best vegetables are selected. Any assortment of vegetables can be used in this recipe.*

1 tbsp. vegetable oil

1 small onion, peeled and sliced

2 cups bite-sized pieces of mixed fresh vegetables**

1 tbsp. fish sauce

1½ tsp. sugar

¼ tsp. pepper

1. In a large skillet or wok, heat oil over high heat for 1 minute.

2. Fry onion over high heat, stirring constantly, for 3 minutes, or until tender.

3. Add mixed vegetables. Cook for 2 to 4 minutes, stirring constantly, until thickest vegetable is crisp-tender.

4. Add fish sauce, sugar, and pepper and stir.

5. Serve hot with rice.

Preparation time: 20 minutes
Cooking time: 10 minutes
Serves 4

* For a more colorful dish, include vegetables of different colors. For green, white, and yellow, use green beans or broccoli, sliced cabbage or cauliflower or mushrooms, and yellow carrots or squash.

** For a quick version of this recipe, use a 10- or 14-oz. can of mixed stir-fry vegetables, drained, instead of the fresh vegetables. If this isn't quite 2 cups, add a bit more from a second can, or add a fresh vegetable or two until you have 2 cups.

Nam Pla Prig

This sauce combines the salty, sweet, and sour tastes that Thai people love. It can be found on every table and is used both as a dip and in place of salt. The Thai sprinkle it on most dishes. Once you discover how good it is, you may want to make a double recipe.

2 cloves garlic, crushed

1 tsp. crushed red pepper flakes

4 tbsp. sugar

2 tbsp. fresh lime or lemon juice, or
    4 tbsp. white vinegar

4 tbsp. fish sauce

2 tbsp. water

1. Combine all ingredients in a small bowl. Stir to dissolve sugar. (If sauce is too salty or too strong, add more water, 1 tablespoon at a time, until it is the desired strength.)

2. Serve at room temperature in individual bowls. (Nam pla prig will keep for up to two weeks refrigerated in a tightly covered glass container.)

Preparation time: 10 minutes
Makes about ½ cup

Sweet and Sour Sauce

1 c. sugar

¼ c. white vinegar

1 tsp. salt

½ c. water

1 tbsp. ketchup

¼ tsp. crushed red pepper flakes

1. In a large saucepan, combine all ingredients. Stir constantly over high heat until sugar dissolves.

2. Serve at room temperature.

Preparation time: 15 minutes
Makes 1½ cups

Cucumber Sauce

1 c. peeled and thinly sliced cucumber*

½ c. white vinegar

1 c. sugar

1 tsp. salt

1. Place sliced cucumbers in a small bowl.

2. In a medium saucepan, combine vinegar, sugar, and salt and bring to a boil over high heat. Stir until sugar dissolves. Remove from heat and let cool, uncovered, to room temperature.

3. Pour sauce over cucumbers immediately before serving.

Preparation time: 15 minutes
Makes 1½ cups

* If you want to remove seeds from the cucumber, slice it in half the long way, then scrape the seeds out with a spoon.

Snacks and Sweets

The Thai are known for their fondness for snacks. No matter how many foods might be offered in the home at mealtime, the Thai cannot resist the snacks sold at food stalls. Street vendors call out to passersby, describing the tasty foods at their stalls and the sauces that go with them. To the Thai, a snack, whether soup or noodles or finger food, is not really food—it is *sanuk*, or fun!

Fresh fruit is the typical sweet in this tropical country, where fruit trees produce much lush fruit. Mangoes, rambutan, bananas, melons of all sorts, mangosteen, papayas, lychee, pineapple, and durian are widely available. Fruit vendors display baskets of ripe fruit in open-air markets. If a cook decides to prepare a dessert, coconut milk and palm sugar, as well as sweet or sticky rice, mung beans, and bananas, are often used.

Filled with onion, bean sprouts, carrots, and meat, Thai spring rolls make a wonderful snack. (Recipe on pages 58–59.)

Thai Spring Rolls / *Poa Pee*

Crispy spring rolls are served at the New Year and for special occasions. Since spring rolls are deep-fried, you must have an adult help you handle the hot oil, which can be extremely dangerous.

3 dried black mushrooms

3½ oz. cellophane noodles or bean thread noodles

1 egg

½ lb. lean ground pork

½ lb. lean ground beef

1 c. peeled and shredded carrots

1 c. fresh bean sprouts, or 1 c. shredded cabbage

½ medium-sized onion, finely chopped

1 tbsp. fish sauce

¾ tsp. ground black pepper

½ clove garlic, finely chopped

1 tsp. sugar

12-oz. package 8-inch-diameter dried rice paper spring roll wrappers

vegetable oil for deep-fat frying—enough to have one inch of oil in bottom of skillet or wok

nam pla prig or sweet and sour sauce for dipping

1. To make the filling, soak black mushrooms in hot water in a small bowl for 15 minutes. Drain well in a colander. Slice mushroom caps thinly and discard the stems.

2. Soak noodles in hot water for 4 to 5 minutes. When soft, drain and cut into 2-inch lengths with a sharp knife or scissors.

3. In a large bowl, beat egg well. Add sliced mushrooms, softened noodles, pork, beef, carrots, bean sprouts, onion, fish sauce, pepper, garlic, and sugar. Mix well. Set aside.

4. To moisten the spring roll wrappers, heat 2 quarts water in a wide pan until hot but not boiling. Take one of the rice paper sheets, holding it by one edge, and dip it in the water for 1 or 2 seconds. The hot water softens it and makes it pliable. Working quickly, take the moistened edge and dip the part you were holding earlier in the water. Be careful. If the rice paper becomes too wet, it tears easily.

5. To form spring roll, place ¼ c. of the filling in center of moistened spring-roll wrapper. Fold bottom edges over filling. Fold in the right and left edges so they overlap. Roll up toward top. Place on a plate with top edge under roll. Cover with moist towel until ready to fry. Preparing about six rolls at a time should work well.

* For a delicious vegetarian version of these rolls, use 1 lb. shiitake or portobello mushrooms, chopped, and ½ cup shredded carrot in place of black mushrooms, pork, and beef.

6. In a large skillet or wok, heat oil over medium heat until it reaches 350°F on deep-fat thermometer. Carefully place 3 rolls in hot oil. Fry slowly for 4 minutes on one side. Turn and fry other side 3 minutes, or until light golden brown. Drain on paper towels. Fried rolls can be kept warm in a 200°F oven.

7. Cut each spring roll into bite-sized pieces. Serve hot with individual bowls of nam pla prig (recipe on page 54) or with sweet and sour sauce (recipe on page 55).

Preparation time: 60 minutes
Cooking time: 60 minutes
Makes 24 spring rolls

Thai Coconut Custard/ Sang Ka Ya

4 eggs

¼ c. brown sugar

¼ c. granulated white sugar

1 c. coconut milk (recipe on page 36)

1 c. thinly sliced winter squash, seeds and rind removed (butternut or buttercup squash or pumpkin can also be used)

1. Preheat oven to 350°F. In a deep bowl, beat eggs well. Add sugars and stir until dissolved. Stir in coconut milk and squash.

2. Pour into a 9 × 9-inch baking pan or a 9- or 10-inch pie plate.

3. Bake custard 45 to 50 minutes until knife inserted in center comes out clean. Serve at room temperature.

Preparation time: 10 to 15 minutes
Cooking time: 45 to 50 minutes (plus cooling time)
Serves 6

Bananas in Syrup/ Glooy Boud Chee

¼ c. sugar

½ c. water

4 firm medium bananas, peeled, halved crosswise, then quartered

⅛ tsp. salt

1½ c. coconut milk (recipe on page 36)

1. In a large saucepan, bring sugar and water to a boil over high heat, stirring constantly. Add bananas and reduce heat to medium. Cook, uncovered, for 8 to 10 minutes, or until bananas are tender.

2. Stir salt into coconut milk. Pour coconut milk over bananas. Serve at room temperature.

Preparation and cooking time: 15 minutes
Serves 4 to 6

Bananas in syrup (top) and Thai coconut custard (bottom) are both sweet treats that make wonderful desserts after a spicy meal.

Holiday and Festival Food

The Thai enjoy many holidays and festivals. They delight in visiting friends and family—or inviting family and friends to come to their home—to celebrate special days. They may watch parades of floats, view brightly lit public buildings, or tour exhibits of beautiful fruits and flowers. But the best part is sharing fun, conversation, laughter, and food.

Any of the recipes in this book could be served at a feast to celebrate a holiday or to mark a festival day. The more people sharing the feast, the greater the variety of dishes Thai cooks will prepare. And if there is a trained carver of garnishes in the family, fruits and vegetables will be carved in the shape of flowers and then used to decorate the serving platters. The recipes that follow are reserved for holidays because they require extra work. On festive occasions, additional family members are on hand to help with food preparation.

Traditional Thai fried noodles are served at holidays—or anytime. (Recipe on pages 64–65.)

Thai Fried Noodles/ Pad Thai

This noodle dish is popular in Thai restaurants all over the world. Most Thai families have their own favorite version. Some cooks cut the noodles in 6- or 8-inch pieces so they will be easier to fry, but the traditional Thai belief is that long, whole noodles bring long life. Since there are lots of steps in making pad thai, ask a parent or older brother or sister to help you.

½ lb. narrow (⅛ inch) rice noodles

3 to 4 tbsp. fish sauce

6 tbsp. granulated sugar

6 tbsp. white vinegar

I tbsp. ketchup (optional)

½ lb. chicken, pork, or shrimp, or a combination

⅓ c. vegetable oil

2 to 3 cloves garlic, finely chopped

2 eggs

4 green onions, sliced

12 oz. fresh bean sprouts (4¾ c.)

¾ c. ground roasted peanuts

red pepper flakes

lime wedges

1. Soften noodles by soaking in water, following directions on package. Drain noodles in a colander. They should be bendable and soft.

2. In a small bowl, mix fish sauce, sugar, vinegar, and ketchup (optional). Set aside.

3. Cut the chicken or pork into pieces about ⅛-inch thick and 1 to 2 inches long. If using shrimp, cut out the black vein along the back of the shrimp.* Leave the tails on the shrimp.

4. Heat a wok or large skillet. Add the oil. Using both hands and hot pads or mitts, carefully tilt the wok so that the oil covers the inside.

5. Add garlic and stir-fry until golden—be careful, it can burn in no time.

6. Add the chicken or pork and stir-fry briefly until pink color is gone. If using shrimp, stir-fry only until they turn pink.

7. Meanwhile, in a small bowl, beat eggs with a fork. Pour eggs into meat mixture in wok and stir lightly to scramble.

8. Add fish sauce mixture and continue stirring.

9. Add the softened noodles. Using a spoon in each hand, toss the noodles lightly to mix in the meat, garlic, and eggs.

10. Add the green onions and ⅔ of the bean sprouts. Cook, tossing mixture gently, until sprouts are tender but still crisp. Turn onto a large warmed platter.** Garnish with the rest of the bean sprouts and the ground peanuts. Pass around little bowls of red pepper flakes and lime wedges so that each person can add the amount they like.

Preparation time: 30 to 40 minutes
Cooking time: 8 to 12 minutes
Serves 4 to 6

* If you use fresh shrimp for this recipe, you may be able to have it peeled and deveined at the grocery store. Otherwise, you can do it yourself. Hold the shrimp so that the underside is facing you. Starting at the head, use your fingers to peel off the shell from the head toward the tail. Then, using a sharp knife, carefully make a shallow cut all the way down the middle of the back. Hold the shrimp under cold running water to rinse out the dark vein.

** To warm the platter, put it in a sink full of warm water. Remove from water and dry the platter just before use.

Galloping Horses (Pineapple Snacks with Pork-Peanut Topping)/Ma Hore

Thai cooks are constantly inventing new finger foods. Since finger foods take more time and work to prepare than most main dishes, they are usually reserved for special occasions. But the work will go fast if you set up a little assembly line with one person placing the fruit on the plate(s), the second topping the fruit with the meat mixture, and the third adding the garnish.

⅓ c. dry-roasted peanuts

2 tbsp. vegetable oil

1 tbsp. minced onions

2 cloves garlic, minced

½ lb. lean ground pork

1 tbsp. sugar

1 tsp. salt

¼ tsp. ground red, white, or black pepper

2 tsp. cornstarch combined with 2 tsp. cold water

72 bite-sized pieces of fresh or canned pineapple, about ½-inch thick and 1 inch across (from 12 precut pineapple rings)

fresh cilantro leaves for garnish

1. Using electric blender or food processor, chop peanuts very finely and set aside.

2. Using a heavy medium-sized skillet, heat oil over medium heat for 1 minute. Add onions and garlic and stir-fry 3 to 4 minutes, until soft but still golden.

3. Add pork and cook, stirring constantly to break up chunks, until no trace of pink remains. Stir in the peanuts, sugar, salt, and pepper.

4. Stir in the cornstarch mixture. Simmer over low heat, stirring occasionally, for 5 minutes, until mixture is thick enough to hold its shape.

5. Lay out pineapple pieces on a platter or two. Top each with 1 teaspoon of the pork filling. Garnish each portion with a cilantro leaf.

Preparation time: 25 minutes
Cooking time: 15 to 20 minutes
Serves 36 (2 snacks each)

Tropical Fruit Dessert

A refreshing do-ahead dessert nice enough for guests.

20-oz. can rambutan or lychees, in syrup, or 15-oz. can mango slices

½ c. coconut milk (recipe on page 36)

2 tbsp. sugar

1 c. canned pineapple chunks, in syrup, chilled

cracked ice (optional)

1. Drain fruit, reserving the syrup. If using rambutan or lychees, cut fruit in half. Chill until serving time.

2. In a little bowl, stir together 1 c. of fruit syrup, coconut milk, and sugar. Stir until sugar is dissolved. Cover this sauce and chill it.

3. Cut pineapple chunks in half.

4. At serving time, divide fruit evenly among 4 large or 6 medium dessert dishes. Pour chilled coconut sauce over fruit.*

Preparation time: 10 to 15 minutes (plus chilling time)
Serves 4 to 6

* If the weather or the room is hot, put ice cubes in a plastic bag and break up the ice. Spoon a few pieces of ice over each dish of dessert.

Holiday Fruit Platter

The Thai delight in bright color and lovely patterns whether in arrangements of fruit for a holiday party, in lengths of shiny silk, or in displays of fresh flowers. You can prepare this buffet dessert quickly with the help of a friend or family member.

5 or more kinds of fresh and/or canned fruit, including lychees or rambutan, watermelon, cantaloupe, honeydew melon, bananas, pineapple, and mango (if you use banana, make fairly large slices, cutting on the slant)

fresh limes for garnish

1 can frozen limeade concentrate, thawed*

*You will have extra limeade concentrate with this recipe. Mix the remaining limeade concentrate with water as directed on the can and serve as a drink.

1. Choose a large platter, one that is big enough to hold a generous amount of fruit.

2. In the center of the platter, make a pile of lychees or rambutan.

3. Divide the platter into sections using pieces of peeled and sliced watermelon about 1 inch wide and 3 or 4 inches long to mark the sections. Cut all the remaining fruit into chunks. If you have a melon baller, scoop the flesh of one of the melons into balls for contrast.

4. Fill in the sections using a different fruit in each for a pretty pattern.

5. Cut limes into thin wedges. Fit the lime wedges around the outer edge of the platter to create a ruffle effect.

6. Pour ⅓ c. limeade concentrate into a 1-c. measuring cup and stir in ⅓ c. water. Using a pastry brush, brush the limeade mixture over the fruit. It will make the fruit shiny and will keep the banana from turning brown.

Preparation time: 30 to 40 minutes
Serves 8 to 10

Index

About the Authors

Supenn Harrison—a native Thai—came to Minneapolis, Minnesota, in 1972, to attend graduate school. She started her first Thai restaurant in 1979 and opened a second in 1983. Her business has grown steadily to a total of seven restaurants, six in the Twin Cities of Minneapolis and St. Paul and one in the nearby city of St. Cloud. Harrison and her husband are parents of two grown daughters. She also finds time to teach Thai cooking, to swim, and to camp.

Judy Monroe, born in Duluth, Minnesota, is a clinical researcher who enjoys Southeast Asian cooking. A graduate of the University of Minnesota, Monroe is also a busy freelance writer and editor. She has written 34 books, many of them for children, and 120 magazine articles, several for national cooking magazines. Her hobbies include reading, gardening, and teaching cooking.

Photo Acknowledgments The photographs in this book are reproduced courtesy of: © Dean Conger/CORBIS, pp. 2-3; © Walter & Louiseann Pietrowicz/September 8th Stock, pp. 4 (both), 5 (both), 16, 28, 33, 34, 39, 40, 44, 47, 48, 53, 56, 61, 62, 69; © John Elk III, p. 6; © John Penisten/Pacific Pictures, p. 10; © Robert Fried, p. 15; © Michael Freeman/CORBIS, p. 24.

Front cover and spine photos: © Walter & Louiseann Pietrowicz/September 8th Stock, back cover © Robert L. and Diane Wolfe.

The illustrations on pp. 7, 17, 30, 31, 37, 38, 42, 43, 45, 46, 50, 52, 55, 59, 65, 67, and 68 and the map on p. 8 are by Tim Seeley.